T0148235

EMMA STREET

CLIFF MCDUFFIE

authorHOUSE®

AuthorHouse™
1663 Liberty Drive
Bloomington, IN 47403
www.authorhouse.com
Phone: 1-800-839-8640

© 2012 by Cliff McDuffie. All rights reserved.

No part of this book may be reproduced, stored in a retrieval system, or transmitted by any means without the written permission of the author.

Published by AuthorHouse   10/11/2012

ISBN: 978-1-4772-1075-8 (sc)
ISBN: 978-1-4772-1076-5 (hc)
ISBN: 978-1-4772-1074-1 (e)

Any people depicted in stock imagery provided by Thinkstock are models, and such images are being used for illustrative purposes only.
Certain stock imagery © Thinkstock.

This book is printed on acid-free paper.

Because of the dynamic nature of the Internet, any web addresses or links contained in this book may have changed since publication and may no longer be valid. The views expressed in this work are solely those of the author and do not necessarily reflect the views of the publisher, and the publisher hereby disclaims any responsibility for them.

EMMA STREET PREVIEW

*The year is 1939 and the family of five children a*nd two adults have moved to a rental property until Dad can find a suitable house to put his family in. The house he finds is on East Emma Street.

A big (to me, later not big enough) house painted an ugly brown sitting on a beautifully shaded street in a middle class section of a small, growing town in west central Florida called Tampa.

DEDICATION

I am dedicating this to my two remaining siblings,
John McDuffie and Rev. Ermalou Roller.
To my sons, Trey and Mike (Wendy) and to my Grandchildren,
Cassidy, Julian and Olive McDuffie.
To my step-sons, Michael and Roger (Nena) Hatfield, and daughter-in-law,
Karen.
Especially to my wife Joyce for putting up with me as I struggled to
finish this.

First Sight

The year is 1939 and the family of five children and two adults have moved to a rental property until Dad can find a suitable house to put his family in. The house he finds is on East Emma Street.

A big (to me, later not big enough) house painted an ugly brown sitting on a beautifully shaded street in a middle class section of a small, growing town in west central Florida called Tampa.

The street is paved with asphalt bricks, as are many streets of that era and there is a canopy of large Oak trees covering the street to make a kind of tunnel as you walked down the sidewalk. Yes there was a sidewalk; not all areas in this town had a sidewalk yet so this must be a fairly good neighborhood. At least we certainly thought so.

My first impression of the new house was a good one as it had a great big Oak tree in the back of the lot just made for boys of five to climb up. There are also orange, tangerine and grapefruit trees.

We have really struck it rich!

As this was the spring of the year there was also a yard full of Oak leaves to be raked up by one five year old.

My second impression of the Emma St. House, as it was to be fondly called in years to come, was one of horror.

As we entered the house to begin cleaning there must have been ten thousand roaches scurrying about! Let me quickly explain that "roaches" in this part of Florida are the two-inch Palmetto Bugs that love to fly at you if disturbed. Apparently the house had not been occupied in some time and as these "bugs" are prone to do, they came in and occupied the house waiting to antagonize its occupants forever. They certainly did an excellent job of that over the next twenty years.

I really have a difficult time remembering exactly how Mom and Dad divided us kids up to sleep as there were three boys and two girls. The girls were both older by two and four years so they probably demanded some separation but in a two bedroom house. I, for the life of me, can not recall where we slept. I do know that the boys had the back bedroom with the bunk beds in it. I was five, then there was three year old John, and Ralph, just one.

Ralph, for the record was called "Cougar" as he was just as quick and elusive at that age as any kid you would ever see!

The girls, Joan (we always had to call her JoAnne) and Clarice were so much older, eight and six respectively, that we boys just kind of ignored them most of this time.

BEFORE EMMA STREET

I do not have much of a recollection of the first house I was aware of on Robeson St in North Tampa about 3 blocks from the Hillsborough River and the community of Sulphur Springs. Mom tells on me about my not ever walking, just getting up and running, everywhere. She could not even keep me in the house. At one time she locked the screen door, we all had screen doors then, but I just got the broom and slipped that latch right out and down the street I went.

Screen doors then had a small hook like lock that slipped into an eye in the door frame. It was not really hard to open I just wasn't tall enough to reach it.

Now this house was only about a block from Nebraska Avenue, which even then, was a relative busy street.

The reason I headed that way was due to the small store there and I would slip in and steal candy bars. I got caught. Yep, a good spanking went with that.

We soon moved to New Orleans Avenue a little closer to town and this was where I can really say that I began to remember things that happened to me and my family.

Now this was what is referred to as a bungalow. It had a porch all the way across the front of the house, an attic and a porte-cochere (that's French for carport) for you to park your car under.

It was here that I associated with my two older siblings in a neighborhood newspaper. I was the sports editor (copies are still available if you are interested and if I can find them again) and we had conned our cousin who was at college to type the paper up for us.

We later learned that our little paper had been sent all over the world as just the cutest thing. It was during this time that my sister, Clarice, enticed me to eat a dirt sandwich. Now I know that not everyone has had the pleasure of dining at midday on two pieces of bread with a healthy packing of loose Florida soil. Quite frankly, I can to this day, still feel that CRUNCH as I naively bit into that rare morsel of food much to the delight of not just Clarice, but of all the kids in the block. After all, this was a treat to see the little guy really get a mouth full.

It was on this street that I had my first gun! Now don't get excited, it was a rubber gun. Not made of rubber but made of wood to look like a pistol, or even a rifle. It had a clothes pin (ask your Grandmother what those are) secured on the handle and you loaded it with rubber bands cut from an inner tube. You may not even know what that is but it went inside your automobile tire and held the air for the tire. One end of the rubber went on the barrel of the pistol and the other was secured with the clothes pin "trigger" on the handle. To release the "bullet" you simply opened the clothes pin with the heel of your hand and the released tension shot the rubber band at a pretty good clip. It would never really hurt you but they did sting. There were many rubber gun battles we waged with our "behind us" neighbors.

A Real Blast

New Orleans was also the street where I learned that when my father told me not to touch something, there was a REAL reason for it.

Dad had bought home a brand spanking new console radio. You know, one of those BIG ones that sat tall on the floor. Dad had plugged the radio in, turned it on, to God only remembers what program, and had left strict instructions to all of us NOT TO TOUCH. Well, I just couldn't stand that and as Dad left the room I, of course, went over reached out and spun the closest knob.

BAROOOOM!!!

I had spun the volume control all the way to L O U D!

Scared the living hell out of me as I fell back on the floor, picked myself up and ran out the front door.

Boy, I don't think the hot water heater on Emma Street ever made me run that fast. Ok the hot water heater will come up later. Right now I was running to save my life. Not just from that thing that "SCREAMED" at me but also because I KNEW that Dad was going to really fix my rear end good. I don't remember exactly what the punishment was but I know to this day I prefer SOFT music!

CUBAN INFLUENCE

This was a really nice neighborhood and we used to hang out at one of the neighbors garage and watch them roll those hand made cigars. That aroma has lingered with me all these many years and I can still picture the old man (probably at least thirty) sitting at his little workbench rolling, pasting and slicing the end off all those cigars. He also spoke a kind of hard to understand English as he was from Cuba, wherever in the world that was.

We also bobbed for apples on Halloween in a great big washtub full of water with apples floating in it. You would have to hold your hands behind your back and try to get an apple by just using just your teeth to bite into it and lift it out of the water. NO HANDS! We also would have all the neighborhood kids over for a costume party then go out from door to door trick or treating. Mom or Dad would always walk along with us just to keep us from getting run over by a car I'm sure.

CATCHING SANTA

I think the best thing I remember about New Orleans Avenue was the Christmas that we almost caught Santa Clause. We had all piled into the car (Dad was selling Pontiac cars then) and gone to see who had Christmas trees up with pretty lights or some or real candles on their trees.

Before we had piled into the car we had very carefully left out for Ole Saint Nick, a nice healthy serving of fresh baked cookies and a great big glass of fresh, cold milk hoping to entice the jolly man to sit a spell. Well it must have worked 'cause as we were going in the front door after a nice ride looking at other peoples trees, we heard the back door slam and sure enough there was a bunch of noise like we had never heard before and then to our utter amazement we heard the definite sound of jingling bells as those tiny reindeer headed for the sky. We knew that it had to be reindeer and Santa because all the cookies were eaten and the milk was gone! Boy o boy that was some Christmas.

I think I got my scooter that year.

THE HEDGES OF EMMA STREET

Well I did kinda get backtracked there so let me go on back over to Emma St. After all it was only about a mile or two away.

The Emma St. House was protected on the West Side and the front by some wonder plants we kids called 'hedge plants'. We don't know to this day what they are really called but they sure came in handy for all kinds of great pretend toys. They also had this little red flower that would pop out all rolled up tight and then one day it would burst open and when that happened, we would pluck it carefully from its holder and suck on the end that had been attached to the plant. What sweet nectar that was. Best of all it never made us sick like some of the other things we put in our mouths. We could always find a nice long piece of 'hedge' to make a long bow out of when we played Robin Hood. If you were careful and let the 'hedge' sticks dry out just right; you could also whittle down the end to a point and shoot your arrows at screeching Blue Jays. You had to be careful when you did that because if you let them get to dry they would break on you as you pulled back on the bow string and it would sure hurt your shooting arm.

HEDGES ON LEGS

As I think back now we always wondered why those 'hedge' plants never got very thick but I guess it was because we were always cutting them down for some game or other or worse yet Mom would make us go out and cut a 'hedge' SWITCH when we had erred somewhat. Now if we had really goofed up, Mom herself would go out and cut a nice, slender OAK switch and blister our bottoms. Now let me tell you something right here, those oak trees are great to climb in but you better believe those tiny little switches could really make a young, healthy boy dance like nobody's business and we didn't have to take dance lessons either. We just did what comes naturally when the oak met the leg. I guess today Mom would be hauled off to court for child abuse but let me tell you. It let us know that there were limitations to what we did and if we "broke the law" we would pay for it. That's a lasting impression

THE PLAY BOX

Now running down the West Side of the house there was about five feet of pure heaven to us boys. This was the stretch of sand (no grass could ever grow with the 'hedge' right there and the next door neighbors house next to that) that we built castles in, farmed, fought naval battles, buried the good silver, and dug tunnels to China. We heard it was down there and all you had to do was dig far enough and these little slant eyed people would come crawling out. Let me tell you, it never worked! Maybe it just got dark too soon and we had to go inside.

Now we didn't always have to go inside just because it had gotten dark! Nosiree!! Many a night we would play hide and seek right on up till nine o'clock when we couldn't see anyone run right by us to be in free. Then we would all go get our special jars and catch the fireflies or lightning bugs. If you got enough of these things in your jar it was like having a pulsing, lighted heart right there in your hand. There were literally thousands of them flying around after dark. We must have done a real good job of catching those little critters cause I sure don't ever see one anymore and I don't live too far from where they all were.

BACKYARD ANTICS

Sometimes after dark, when it was too hot to go sit inside the house or if the Green Hornet or The Thin Man or Fibber Magee and Molly or Duffy's Tavern or Lux Radio Theater or Amos and Andy or one of those great shows wasn't on, we would carefully, under the watchful eye of Mom, make a circle of rocks in the back yard and light a bonfire. That was really some fun to sit out near to ten o'clock at night and tell those spooky ghost stories. We would even cut ourselves a nice 'hedge stick', shave off the bark and slide a hot dog over that thing to burn in the fire. For desert we, of course, would roast marsh mellows. Sometimes, if we had a mind to, we would dress up in our best Indian costumes and do our best Indian dance around the fire, complete with tomahawk and war chants. The charred logs made the best war paint along with the pilfered lipstick from our sisters hoard of junk stuff'.

With all the cigar manufactures in Tampa it was easy to get one of the large wooden boxes, they shipped tobacco in, to use in the back yard for a play house or whatever you wanted to do with it. They were fairly large and a young boy my age could stand in one and just about peer over the top. I guess they must have been about 4 ft. by 8ft. and about 4 ft. tall I can only remember having one of those and we must have used it for about everything: forts, ships and train engines. When we had just about destroyed that poor box we could remove the wooden slates and make all kinds of things from them. Like scooters, ladders, wagons, and stilts. We had to do this as there was little money for toys. We just made our own.

BATTLES GALORE

That backyard was definitely our battlefield and many scars exist today from battles waged back there. Some physical but many more mental, such as the day I climbed up the dead Tangerine tree. When I got to the top, which must have been fifty feet at least (more honestly like fifteen feet), that sucker snapped off right at the base and I had the ride of my life in a gentle arch to the ground, with little ole me still sitting in top of that tree.

In those days it was not uncommon to wring a chicken's neck and then dress it down in the back yard. Well as kids will do, we soon found a way to make an exciting process out of this. One day, just after one of us had wrung a hen's neck, we accidentally dropped it and to our fascination that hen took off running around the yard with its neck hanging to one side and us kids rolling in the grass laughing like crazy people at the sight. Needless to say we very often "dropped" the chickens after that, particularly when someone was visiting we wanted to impress. That I'm sure must have left some kind of mental scar.

BROTHERLY LOVE

Now what I am going to relate will, I'm sure, embarrass the fool out of my brother but we are talking scars and I'm sure he still carries this one around with him. In order to climb that big Oak in the back yard we had nailed "boards" (anything flat, wide enough and thick enough to hold a kid) up on the side of the tree to the first limb which was about twelve feet off the ground to act as our ladder. Now one fine summer day as I waited to climb up after my brother, I remembered that he really hated to be tickled and as he grabbed the top rung of the ladder, I unmercifully began tickling him. Here he was hanging from that top rail by his hands, feet kicking out in the air, laughing like a fool, hollering "Quit! You'll make me wet my pants!" Well, well now what do you suppose this loving brother did? You're right! I kept right on tickling and sure enough he wet his pants. Just like he said!

Now that leaves scars.

This same brother was the one watching me throw a rock up into the tree to dislodge my homemade parachute. Yup! You guessed it. He stood right there and watched that rock fall on his head! That's the physical side.

LITTLE SISTER

I think I've jumped ahead a little too far here so I'm going to back up just a few months. It was some time just after we moved into this house (about a year) that my little sister came along and she must have surely been brought by that stork that everyone talks about because I never saw my mom get fat like the ladies do today when they are pregnant. But I know she came to live with us because later on my brothers and I would torment her something awful, just having fun, and she never went away so we just kept her. Besides, she was just as pretty as a little girl could possibly be. She still is even though she's grown up and preaching. We must have started her out in that direction because I'm sure she must have prayed hard at night that we wouldn't do anymore of those crazy things to her.

There was also the prank we pulled on her which I know must have left scars on her for life. Ermalou did not like spiders and we had these mean looking wolf spiders all over the place.

My brother John and I found some small springs, took a small ball and covered it with something to make it look furry, then placed it over the door jam, attached to a string, to Ermalous bedroom. We then called her and as she opened the door that thing fell and jiggled right in front of her face. Scarred the devil out of her. Of course her brothers were rolling on the floor laughing.

DAD'S GONE

In the fall of 1941, just before the Japs did that dastardly deed on Pearl Harbor, our very tight knit family was hit by a different disaster, which left mental scars on all of us. Some of those scars we are still trying to cope with to this day.

Our Dad died.

One day he just went off to work and dropped dead on the job from 'natural causes'. I know that because when I grew up I got a copy of the death certificate and it said it right there under cause of death, 'natural causes'. I've never been able to find out exactly what he did die of and believe you me I have tried. I draw a complete blank about this time in our lives.

I do not know if it is an escape mechanism or if I honestly was just too young to retain that in my memory bank but for what ever reason I do not remember Dad dying or the funeral or anything about that time.

We would never again go for rides on Sunday ending up in Sulphur Springs to get an ice cream cone or a Doctor Pepper, which made your mouth sting. I would never again be given a quarter to run down to the store to get my dad two packs of Lucky Strikes. I well remember the cough drops Dad used. They were not the normal "Smith Brothers" black, good tasting ones, but came in a little metal box. I do not remember what they tasted like but we all would vie for the little metal box. It was used to store all kinds of kids treasures in.

I would no longer be going with dad to the Friday night boxing matches at the Armory (to this day I love to watch the boxing matches) nor would we be able to tool around in the yellow convertible Dad would bring home from the job. It even had a rumble seat, which was real cool to ride in.

Dad was gone, Mom took over.

Then the Japs bombed Pearl Harbor and World War II broke out and of course we all trained our thoughts on making it through the 'Big One'.

BIKE IN THE ATTIC

After Dad died I could never remember the actual event. I knew he was in Heaven but there were times that I wasn't sure and thought that he would come back and bring me the bike I wanted so much.

I wanted a bike so bad and even started to think that if I could get into the attic of our house there would be one up there just for me that someone had forgotten.

The problem with that thinking was that no matter how hard I tried to find a way into the attic there just wasn't any opening I could get into in order to see what was up there.

This one fantasy kept coming back the whole time I was in grade school. Eventually I bought my own bike and never had those thoughts about one in the attic again.

GUAVA WARS

I failed to mention that the Emma Street House had a garage, which set on the back of the property and was only accessible through the alley, which ran the full length of the block. The alley was our main street as there usually wasn't any traffic after the garbage truck went through. You need to know about that alley as it most definitely plays a big part in our neighborhood relations training. The garage was made of corrugated tin and very quickly became our clubroom, hide out and play yard during rains and used for just about everything except a car! The floor was sand and I do recall many hours spent catching 'doodlebugs'! You may well remember those tiny little creatures that would dig into the ground and leave a cone shaped hill. We used to catch those things just to watch them do their thing. If I recall correctly we probably made a game of this also. As you may have gathered by now, we all developed great imaginations due simply to the fact that we had to come up with some way to make the days go by. The garage had been built directly under the Oak tree so we could climb the tree, straddle the peak of the garage and survey almost all of our end of the block. This would give us time to see the neighborhood bully coming so we could gracefully skedaddle into the house and not have to confront the "enemy". The garage roof also provided us with a great place to jump down from. No matter if you landed right on top of somebody when you jumped. We always yelled "Watch out" so if anyone got hit it sure wasn't our fault. This also became an excellent place to throw overripe Guavas which were plentiful long enough in the year to get all the bellyaches you may want in one summer. Boy were those Guavas good! I can still see those light yellow objects smashing into the back of the guys who lived behind us as they scurried away from trying to steal our toys, not knowing we were right there on top of the garage waiting so we could toss those Guavas. They would break open on contact, if you had picked carefully, and splash all over your "enemies'" back! If you didn't pick carefully you could very well have them running down your arm as you tried to throw them. See we really had to exercise some form of judgment, even if it was to the ripeness of our artillery shells. For you folks who have never eaten Guavas—you just haven't lived; and if you have never been hit in the backside with an 'over ripe' one, then you don't know what it's like to stink!!

SCHOOL, FIRST GRADE

Even though we boys had our hands full helping fight the war, on the home front life went on and it came that time for me to begin getting ready for the big day: that first day of school. I really wanted to go to school mainly because when you started to school you could start wearing long pants. I know I didn't mention this earlier but little boys all wore short pants. Only on Sunday and special occasions did you wear long pants. I well remember that first day of school when I walked into the first grade room. There were these great big letters printed on lined paper hanging across the top of what we came to know as the blackboard. They were real neat looking letters. Little did I know that within a short time I would be required to LEARN those things. I will never, ever, forget that teacher, Ms. McClain. I only use Ms. here because I had no idea if she was married or did I care. I do know that she was a very attractive lady with gray hair and I would sure do anything she asked me to do. I hope I did over the next year, at least

I passed first grade. That was a start.

I am told that I got into trouble for talking or something but I don't remember that at all. I do remember having to go to the principal's office once in the second grade for shooting spitballs. If you've never done that let me tell you how. All you need is a small piece of paper folded up tightly and a rubber band to propel it at your "victim". The folded paper is bent to make a "V" and you place that on one side of the rubber band, put the rubber band around your thumb and forefinger, pull back on the paper and let it fly. Now I may have done that but that particular day I was NOT guilty and took the blame for the kid sitting right behind me.

What was really nice was that there were some real cute girls in my class. I still know some of them and they do talk to me so I must not have been too bad that first year. I really liked doing those A B Cs. When it was time to take an afternoon nap I would always get a book to look at because I just could not go to sleep when there was sunshine out side. I still have a problem sleeping in the daytime but I will admit it is not quite as hard to catch forty winks today as it was then.

RECESS

You do, I am sure, remember that I have two older sisters, so now that I had started school I began to get the "Oh yes I taught his sister last year. I hope he does just as well as she did." Well I can't say that I did but it never really bothered me because even at that age I was fairly certain of myself. Timid and reserved but not afraid to do what I had to do. There is what I remember about the first grade: we all went to this great big room for lunch and went through a line to get our food. I don't know how much we had to pay for the food but we did have to give them some money. We also had to sit with our class and when we got through eating we would all go out to the playground to run some of the excess energy off. Guess that was a way to help the teacher keep us under control after lunch.

We did have a recess period in the morning and in the afternoon to play kick ball, hopscotch, baseball, keep away, jump rope and, if we were lucky, play in the sand.

MEASLES

It seems to me that I was in the 4th grade when I came home one day not feeling to good. Maybe just a kid thing. Upset stomach, a little headache.

The next morning however I was breaking out all over with these little red dots like I had been bitten by ants all over my body.

Measles, Mom said and sure enough I was home for about a week in bed. The room was darkened so my eyes would not be affected and I could not go outside for that whole time.

On the front porch the Health Dept. made us put up a sign that said **Quarantined due to MEASELS**. That kept other kids from playing with anyone else in the family till the waiting period was over.

Now in a family of six kids it happens. One down 5 to go. We were off limits for quite some time I imagine.

Not only did we all go through the measles but whopping cough, smallpox and what ever else came down the pike or maybe I should say in the school.

It was no fun but we lived through it with no scars from smallpox or nothing that we know of from the other childhood diseases known to us then.

We did get a smallpox vaccination and some of us had a light case due to the shot. But no disfiguring thank goodness.

The only disease we were really afraid of was polio. It was the one that frightened everyone then. We had a couple of family friends that came down with it but lived through it slightly crippled.

At that young age I wanted to be a doctor and find the cure for polio.

Fortunately the cure was found before I got out of high school.

I didn't become a doctor anyway.

OUR HAUNTED HOUSE

I guess the best part about going to school was getting out in the afternoon! It was only about five blocks to our house from the school so we walked both ways to school. I don't recall ever seeing a school bus until I got to junior high. On the way home we had to pass by an old house that no one had lived in for a long time. At least not as long as any of us or our older brothers or sisters could remember so that must have been a really long time. Anyway we all KNEW that old house was HAUNTED and it was not disrespectful to walk on the other side of the street as you went by. That old house is still standing at this writing and I do not know if anyone has ever lived in it! This was also the place you kept away from on Halloween night. Just to be safe.

MR. MURRAY

The family next door, the Murray's, were good friends. There was a husband and wife and a daughter.

The daughter was a very pretty red head.

Fortunately at that time I wasn't that interested in girls as she was about 3 years older than me.

Mr. Murray was a really interesting person and I took to him quickly. I have no idea what he did for a living but he did ride a motorcycle and that made him different. He had an old Indian motorcycle and sometimes as he came down the street he would stand up on the seat and drive it standing up.

That was really wild for us kids. Mr. Murray loved to rebuild old cars and always had one or two in his back yard that he was working on. Old cars then had woodwork inside and he would very carefully remake broken wooden parts. This may be where I begin to like wood carving as I would help him, or at least I thought I was helping him, work on those cars. Mr. Murray was also the first adult that took me fishing. I do remember that event as he rented a boat and loaned me his casting reel. I, of course, knew absolutely nothing about casting and soon had enough backlash to last me the rest of my life. I remember catching one small fish that we tossed back to let it grow.

Once I became old enough and the new spinning reels came out I went to them very quickly as they do not give you the backlash I never could seem to learn to control.

Some years later the Murray's were divorced and Mrs. Murray and Margaret remained living next door until I left for college. I only saw the daughter one time after that when I was in my 30's when she got on an elevator at the same time as me.

Nature Class

A very important item here is that one of our across the street neighbors had a few cows that we could watch him milk in the afternoon. It was real fun to watch him drive them home.

After he got them in his barn he would wash their udders off and milk them.

Often, just to give us a show, he would squirt a kitten in the mouth with the milk or squirt it on our bare feet.

SOD PITCHERS

It seems to me that it was about this time that the county had decided to pave the Street, which we had to walk down to get to school. That was not such a big deal but they were going to pave it with a new stuff called asphalt. I don't know if asphalt was new to everyone else or not but it sure was to us. The big road working equipment was the topic of conversation after school for quite sometime.

Once the street was paved, we found out real quick that we had better not walk on it too long if the sun had been beating down because you would sink into the ashalt and go home with tarred feet. I do believe they perfected it somewhat by now. It was the same street, while they were preparing the road bed, that we boys would get our pitching arms in shape by standing on the large mounds of hard dirt pushed to the side of the road, eyeball a palm sized clump of dirt and watch for an approaching car. Then quick as a cat, we would reach down, grab the clump of dirt and unerringly smack it against the side of the car and haul off running as fast as we could to hide in the Oak tree just in case someone came looking for us. No one ever did but we had to be cautious. Don't even know if it ever helped our pitching arm but to this day I still jog and my brother set a state record for the mile in high school.

LITTLE FIGHTER

My brother, John, two years younger, was blessed with the curliest blond hair you ever saw on a boy and like most of us in the family had beautiful blue eyes. This combination was not bad in itself but my mother decided not to cut his hair. As it grew long it the most beautiful curls you ever saw hung down his back. He would have been the envy of any little girl. Then, little boys wanted long pants but I never knew one that wanted long curly hair. Not back then and particularly not my brother! He would be out playing in the front yard about the time school was let out and as all the older kids came by they kidded him about being a little girl. Now believe me that got his temper up and we would have at least one good fight a week from the "little girl'.

KRAZY KIDS

We had a family living next door that was just half our size, two girls and a boy. We of course became real friendly with them as people did in those days. The oldest girl was a beautiful blond with the prettiest smile you ever saw and really liked to use it. Her sister, a little younger, was studious looking but would have been my choice of a girl friend if I were even thinking about girls then. Then there was Bobby. Bobby was about my age and we really hit it off. He also was crazy.

Well not really but he sure did some crazy things. Like the time they had some large sewer pipes in his back yard that we could play in. Don't know what they were there for but we did play in them and then one day Bobby got this great idea. He crawled inside, turned around, started a fire then crawled to the other end and started another fire BEFORE he crawled out. Needless to say we heard his screaming and put out the fires without any one being hurt.

Another time we were playing inside his house and good old Bobby challenged me to try his dad's Red Man chewing tobacco. Well it sounded ok and I had seen his dad chew it and it didn't seem to bother him so I accepted the challenge and plopped a great big plug into my mouth. That plug was not in my mouth more than two seconds when I was spitting it all over the floor and anything else which might have been in the way. I cannot for the life of me understand why people chew that horrible tasting stuff. I guess if my mom reads this she will learn for the first time about my introduction to tobacco. I don't think it will surprise her that it was Bobby that gave me that introduction.

Bobby also had a great big dog that was just a real sweetheart around all us kids. Well not always. One day Bobby and I were involved in one of our games in the front yard. This one required that we chase each other around one of those large Oaks I mentioned. Apparently Bobby's dog thought that I was going to do harm to Bobby as he suddenly lunged across the yard and took a big bite of my rear end.

This scarred the daylights out of both of us. Of course the skin of my fanny was bruised as well as bleeding so they had to put the poor dog to sleep to make sure it didn't have rabies.

The Animal Control Department, if that's what it was called then, said no rabies.

By that time I had already taken those horrible rabies shots and to this day I cringe when someone wants to poke me with a needle. It was a lovely dog and I sure wish they had not had to do put it to sleep. We all felt that the poor dog, Oscar, was just protecting his master from someone who he thought was going to harm him.

Somewhere along about this time we discovered how to make real bombs! We would find two same sized bolts and a nut to fit. Then we would carefully remove the ends of several kitchen matches. You remember those with the large red and white end you could strike anywhere. We would put the nut on one of the bolts, then place the "explosive" end of the matches we had removed in the cup formed by the nut, then screw the other bolt into the nut. Now when you threw this down, on it's end, on a hard surface like the sidewalk it would explode. You could also use those caps that everyone bought to shoot in our cap pistols.

A wonder we never got killed doing this.

I Scream You Scream

One thing during the summer months we could all look forward to was the tingling of the ice cream vendor's bells as he road his bicycle pushing the vendor cart down the bumpy asphalt brick street. It was a sound you could well hear in the back yard and when we did we would run for our pocket change or go ask Mom for a dime for ice cream. My favorite was the vanilla cream covered with chocolate on a stick. Also I liked cups of vanilla or butter pecan. In the really hot days an orange or strawberry Popsicle would hit the spot. Those were fun to get because as the cold treat begin to melt the cold water would drip on your stomach and that felt good. Also if you saved enough of the sticks then you could make toys out of them and of course we were always looking for ways to make things to play with.

After the war the ice cream vendor begin coming around with his cart attached to a motor scooter and then ultimately it changed in to a small van with windows on the side to dispense the treats from. That kind of took the thrill off since we no longer heard the tinkling bells

ICE MAN

The thought of ice cream brought to mind another event that we had happening for some time when we first moved to Emma Street: the ice man delivering ice.

As there were very few electric refrigerators at that time, we had an ice box in the kitchen where we kept things like milk and meat. There was not as many items we had that needed refrigeration as we have today so the box did not have to be very large. There was a space for ice and then another for your cooling goods.

The ice man would come around about once a week in a large truck with huge blocks of ice in the back. The man would cut the size block you wanted and bring it in your house and put it into the ice box. He would know how much you needed as you would place a sign on the porch with letters he could see from the street. The sign would be a large paper square with 25, 50, 75 or 100 pounds printed on the outside of the square in large bold numbers. You would hang the sign on a nail and the number on top of the sign would be the amount of ice you wanted that day.

Of course we kids loved for the truck to come as you could always get some ice chips to cool you off on a hot, Florida summer day.

WWII Again

The war over seas was going pretty strong by now and we were busy saving tin cans and other stuff for the war effort. There were even movie theatres that would exchange tickets for a number of tin cans.

We would stay glued to the radio at night to get the latest war news and also to listen to the wonderful programs that would bring us stories about the war such as the Lux Radio Theatre. The next day we would have to play out all of these scenes with our own variations of the script. I was pretty hung up on the aircraft being used in the war effort and could identify most of the more famous planes: the P40 "Flying Tiger", the P39, the F4 Corsair, the P51 Mustang, the B17 (of course), B25 & 26, the various dive bombers that the navy used to sink submarines.

With Mac Dill Army Air Base (yeah, it was still Army Air Corp then) and Drew Field right in our own back yard we often saw many of these planes in our own skies. With my interest in aviation, you can well imagine how excited I got one day as literally hundreds of fighter planes flew over our yard. Headed for some great battle, somewhere. The old Oak tree in the back yard became our B17 and we bombed many German and Japanese ships and cities from high over-head. Towards the end of the war we kept hearing about a new bomber which was to replace the wonderful 'Flying Fortress" B17.

One day as I was at recess at school I heard this loud, different sound overhead and looked up to see the largest bomber one person could imagine. It was the brand new B29. My gosh that thing was HUGE. It seemed to be flying so slow that I couldn't understand how it stayed in the air.

AIR RAIDS AND RATIONS

Well, of course, we went on to win that war and my family did not lose any loved ones to fighting that I know of, so I guess we were very lucky. Some of the many war effort projects we could practice right at home like painting the top half of car headlights black so they didn't show from the air.

Air raid warnings sounded at all times of the day and we would have to get under something like a desk at school. The government rationed food such as sugar, & butter. Butter!

That jarred my memory of the first margarine that came out. Boy was it ever messy to take that big glob of what looked like lard, pop the coloring vial and mix that stuff up! We all knew it wasn't butter but we were helping the war effort so it didn't seem so bad. Gasoline, of course, was rationed and as we did not own a car, it was an experience when one of our relatives would drive to town and we would get to go with them to sit in line to get gas. If you didn't have that little ration sticker on your windshield you were out of luck. Depending on what you did for a living, the gas ration sticker on your car had a big letter on it. A, B or C I think were the ones I saw the most of. This determined the amount of gas you could get at one filling.

WASH BOARDS AND TUBS

As most kids did then, we wore "dungarees" which are referred to as "jeans" today.

We children were expected to help with the wash as Mom was working most of the time. To accomplish this chore we had a bench in the back yard under the kitchen window and under the outside water faucet. On this bench were three large, galvanized wash tubs. We would wash clothes in the first tub with soap, then use the other two tubs for rinsing. Using the washboard was bad enough but having to wring out clothes, especially "dungarees", was a real muscle developer. We would have to keep emptying and refilling each tub to accomplish this chore.

Lost Money

It was about this time I created a very touchy situation. I have always been very careful with money, particularly other peoples. One summer day that I shall remember forever. Mom gave me the grocery list and asked me to go down to Paul's grocery store and get the food for the week. Along with the list I was handed a $5.00 bill. Now in those days that was a lot of money and not only was I pleased to be asked to go to the store all by myself but that I was being entrusted with a fortune. Now Paul and all us McDuffies were on very good terms as most people were back then, with our grocer so Paul helped me reach those items I couldn't. Better yet he let me operate the long stick with the little thing on the end, which you could close around something on the top shelf and bring it right on down to you as if you were six feet tall. When I finished shopping I reached into my pocket to pay Paul. NO MONEY!

Paul said that he would hold the groceries while I went back home to see if I had left the money there, which I very quickly did to no avail. So I had to tell Mom. I then went very slowly back to the store looking all over the street and side-walk for that $5.00 bill. When I got to the store I turned around and walked back to the house on the other side of the street just in case it had blown across the road. NO MONEY! Now I really was in tears as I headed back to the store to tell Paul to put the groceries back on the shelf as I had lost all of our money and we couldn't afford groceries that week. About half way to the store a bolt out of the blue hit me and I knew exactly where that money was. Right there in my WATCH POCKET where I had hid it so no one would find it or I couldn't possible loose it. How happy a kid I was that I had found that money.

Neighborhood Witch

The neighbor's two doors down from us were and old couple, at least 30 or 40 years old. She was a nurse and we all thought that she was really just married to that nice old man to get his money because she was our WICKED WITCH OF THE WEST. She was always hollering at us and sending notes to our moms about things that we would never admit to. So it was no wonder that on a Halloween night we really pulled the BIG trick on her. You know, the one where you get some fresh, I mean really fresh, cow manure from the field, put it in a bag, gently place it in front of the door, set it afire, ring the bell and RUN. It sure was fun to watch her try to stamp out that smelly fire. I don't think that woman thought too highly of us anyway and that sure didn't help matters any.

Broken Nose

One thing that happened while I was in the fourth grade will remain with me for the rest of my life. We were at recess (that was the time allowed for playing outside) and were playing our daily game of "at war". The playground included a very large field that was nothing but good OLE Florida sand. You know, that white stuff that looks like it came from the beach. I was advancing on the enemy when I got 'shot'. It just happened that there was a rather large saw horse right in front of me left there by the janitor. As I begin to fall forward it made sense to me to fall on the sawhorse rather than on the hot sand. Well I did hit that saw horse just right so that I rolled over it and it landed right on my nose. Yep! Hurt like the dickens and blood just flew every where. My big sister, Joan, was appointed to hold a handkerchief over the bleeding nose and escort me, on the 15th Street bus, to the doctor in downtown Tampa. I bled profusely all the way to the doctor's office where he stopped the bleeding and sent me home. For some reason the doctor did not set my nose and it was only many years later when I was in the real army and had it broken again did it get set correctly. Oh, I wasn't advancing on the enemy when I got it broken the last time. I was playing basketball in the base gym and took a hard, direct pass that hit me right in the nose and I knew immediately that it was broken.

HOMEMADE TOYS

Another way we had of entertaining ourselves was to find two boards about the same length and thickness, labor over sawing out two triangles and nailing one to each board and walking around on our stilts. Quite often falling flat on our fanny when the foot hold broke loose. We also would take a large can, lay it on its side and stomp our foot into it to make a kind of horseshoe that made a clanking sound when you walked down the side walk. Another form of entertainment was to take one of our skates apart and fasten the wheels onto a plank and make a scooter out of it.

Of course we always were making bows for when we played cowboys and Indians.

GO FLY A KITE

In March of most years it is fairly windy like everywhere else and a good time to take to the air with our kites.

If we were lucky we would save up our pennies and buy a kite for about ten cents. Of course you would have to assemble the kite yourself but that wasn't a real problem at all.

Kites then were made of a very thin paper with cross sticks and came with enough string to make the bow in the back of the kite. You had to provide your own string to fly these.

There was a vacant lot behind our house that gave us enough running room to get our kites in the air and then it pretty much was just learning to keep it away from the electric lines and trees that were all around.

Once high enough, the kite would catch the wind and really pull the cord from your hand as it took off higher and higher.

Most of the time we would have our kite cord wrapped on a stick so we would have the stick as a handle to hold the kite steady with. Without that stick you could very easily get burned by the cord playing out. Kites then were really not all that fantastic to look at. They may have had designs on them or a Captain Marvel or such figure but that really didn't matter to much when the thing was hundreds of feet in the air.

Getting them down was sometimes tricky as the wind would shift and often it would just slam you into a neighbors tree. It's possible that there are still kites stuck in trees from way back then, probably not but I would like to think so.

Often, when we were really feeling frisky we would find an old safety razor blade, attach it to the tail of our kite and see if we could cut the cord of another kite. When and if that happened, that kite would take off into the wild blue yonder and we would never see that one again.

As often happened our kite would get ripped by a tree limb and the paper would be torn but the frame would still be good. If this happened we would strip the paper, go get some left over Christmas tissue wrapping and airplane glue and replace the paper. It always worked just as good as a new one.

There were times when we didn't have the ten cents to buy a kite that we would simply construct one from scratch. The biggest problem in doing that was to find cross sticks that were limber enough to bend with the wind. If they were too stiff then about the time you got your kite a couple of hundred feet up in the air the cross member would snap in two and your kite would fall to the ground like a wounded sparrow.

FROGS FROM HEAVEN

Now this is one event that really sticks out in my memory simply because I have never seen it happen again.

In tropical Florida it was not uncommon to get a hard rain every summer afternoon. This was always looked forward to as it would cool the evening down and make sleeping a little easier as NO ONE had air conditioners then.

This particular rain was not that much different and started coming down about four or five in the afternoon. After about five minutes of playing in the rain we begin to get hit by something bigger than rain drops. It was actually raining small frogs! Man they were every-where and hopping like crazy when they hit the ground. You couldn't walk without crushing a dozen under you foot at one time. This was so weird. Of course we all ran inside to get out of the downpour of frogs. The next day the streets were covered with dead frogs run over by cars and the smell was not pleasant at all.

Later in life I found that this does happen from time to time and is caused by the new-born frogs being sucked from the swamps by up drafts and then dropped from the clouds along with normal rain water. Strange but true, really strange to a youngster.

GRAND PARENTS

I think it is appropriate here to tell you something about my grandparents who lived in a small community outside Tampa called Brandon. Granddaddy was a Methodist minister who had come to Florida from Alabama when ministers still were circuit riders in the late 1800's. He was a fairly tall, large boned man, bald with a fringe just over the ears and wore glasses. He was very gruff and stern—given to pointing his finger while in the pulpit. Grandmother was a small, delicate looking, (which she wasn't) woman. The real image of a grandmother complete with her hair tied up in a knot on the back of her head. She could cook up a storm and really loved to work in her flower garden. On several occasions I would go out to grandmothers' for a week in the summer to mow the yard (with one of those heavy rotary mowers you had to really work just to push), chase chickens, churn butter and eat her fantastic cookies.

Granddaddy, being the preacher, would always say the blessing before each meal. At breakfast he would also read from The Upper Room a thought for the day followed by about a five or ten minute "blessing" which we always thought was a sermon due to the length and subject matter of it. Somehow "Mither", as he called grandmother, kept the food hot through all this preparation and it really made it taste better because of the anticipation caused by the good smells.

My grandparents were in their seventies at that time and when Grandpa went to sleep he really would saw those logs. I stayed up one night for almost two hours scared to death because I thought there was a hog in the house and it just turned out to be Granddaddy snoring.

There were only two vices that Granddaddy had that I knew of. One was playing dominoes, which he did at length when he wasn't preparing his sermon or visiting his "flock".

Looking back, those summers were really wonderful except for Granddaddy's other vice: driving. He did not like to be behind anyone on the road and would speed up just to pass the car in front of him. He also did not like for anyone to pass him so he would speed up when someone would make the mistake not realizing that they were trying to pass the Rev. George Washington Sellers, Gods servant, which just wasn't allowed. Grandpa also liked to make little things out of wood, that would dance on the end of a stick or go around when the wind blew. That must have been where I got my love of working with wood through being with him in that great big garage with all those neat tools and the smell of freshly worked wood. I don't think we ever got into to much trouble at Grandma's because they kept us busy during the day and we would go to sleep very quickly once the sun went down.

Granddaddy also built the first solar collector I every saw. It was on the north side of the house along the fence facing south and must have been eight feet by twenty feet. This was used to heat water. There was a water tank next to it that must have held a hundred gallons as it was so large. This was in the middle '40's so Grandpa was way ahead of the times.

At Thanksgiving each year all my mothers nine brothers and sisters, who could make it, along with their children, would gather at grandma's house.

The table would be set with all kinds of delicious food, which we couldn't get at until granddaddy had given his "sermon" and this was always a long one. This was about the only time I saw most of my cousins but we looked forward to it each year. We would pretty much do the same thing at Easter, but that of course always included going to hear grandpa preach, in the church, not at the table.

AUNTS AND UNCLES

I need to include here some mention of one of my mother's Sisters, Erma, who would help us out from time to time. She was a music teacher from Frostproof, Florida and taught my sisters how to play our big upright piano. She would hit them on the knuckles with a ruler if they struck the wrong key. One practice piece I have deeply imbedded in my memory is Claire de Lune, which was played over and over, and over. Aunt Erma was a red head with the temper to go with it and was always correcting us with one of those little Oak switches, which were so handy. I well remember the last time she switched me. She was chasing me around the bedroom when I jumped on the bed, yanked the switch from her hand and wielding it over my head said "That's the last time you're going to switch me." She never mentioned this episode to my mother that I know of and we got along fine from then on. Aunt Erma's husband, Uncle Harry (Erma and Harry Flood of Frostproof Fl.), was an Englishman with a bad leg, which was locked at the knee and caused him to walk with a swinging gait. Uncle Harry always saw the humor in things and really had us kids believing that a gator had bitten him on the leg and made it stiff. He and my aunt owned some orange groves near Frostproof. Uncle Harry was at one time elected as Mayor of Frostproof and held office until it was determined that he was not an American citizen and could not hold public office. I later learned that he got his citizenship and had been legally re-elected mayor.

He was also, or at least he told us this, the first white man to view the Seminole Indians green corn dance. He had become friendly with Chief Billy Bowlegs and regularly visited the Seminole reservation in south Florida. Uncle Harry taught me how to make bead work like the Indians and started my interest in Native Americans which I still have. For several summers we would spend a week or two in Frostproof, swimming in Lake Moody, playing with Uncle Harry's "pet" spiders and staying clear of the alligator he kept in the yard. Besides the orange grove Uncle Harry also raised okra and lady finger bananas. Now the bananas we ate with no problem but my aunt loved to steam okra and if you've eaten steamed okra you know how slimy it is. We kids just could not stand to eat it. We were made to however by the threat of a paddling, to eat it. Aunt Erma also subscribed to the National Geographic magazine and one room of their house must have had a thousand of them in it. Now you can just imagine what pictures we boys liked the most. Even though we hardly knew where Africa was we sure liked how the women dressed there with just a cloth around the lower half of their body. We kept an eye out for Aunt Erma while "reading". One of my uncles on Mom's side of the family was the Sheriff in Miami (or at least we thought so) and when he would come to town he would always take us to one of the best Spanish restaurants: The Las Novedadas. That was always a pleasure and we did like his stories.

My Aunt Erma would always take us to Morrison's in downtown Tampa that served buffet style. She loved to say I don't care how much you get but you have to eat all that you get. I liked Morrison's because they had Colored waiters that would pick your tray up at the end of the buffet line and take it to your table. They wore white gloves and always were just as pleasant as could be expected. I really hated it when Morrison's moved from downtown and you had to carry your own tray. Being waited on always made me feel special.

GEORGIA CLAN

Since my father had died so early we hardly got to know his family as they lived in Georgia and that was a long way away. From time to time cousins from Georgia would come down to visit for a few days. One visitor I remember very well was "Mac" who was very hard headed and would not pay attention to what we would tell him. One day I think we helped him change his mind. I am sure you know that Florida is full of oranges, grapefruit, lemons, limes, kumquats and citrus in general. On this day, most of us kids were in the back yard playing when "Mac" came to the back screen door and proceeded to tell us that he was going to eat this big orange he had in his hand rind (skin) and all. Well we immediately warned him that his "orange" was not an orange at all but a very large orange colored lemon and he shouldn't bite into it unless he was prepared to pucker up for at least 15 minutes.

As we knew he would "Mac" said in his best Georgia Drawl "This ain't no lemon. It's a orange". We warned him again to no avail.

"Mac" took as big a mouthful as he could get his mouth around of that "orange". The look on his face remains with me until this day. One of "Oh my God what have I bitten into". As he puckered up from that extremely tart lemon we all rolled on the ground laughing at him. He may still be puckered up as far as I know from that lemon.

My two older sisters and I did ride the train to Abbeville, Georgia the summer after my dad died. That was where he was from and my grandparents there had a great big farm. We rode all night on that train so we did not get to see much countryside and it was hard sleeping with the train swaying on the tracks with a clickity click. My granddaddy McDuffie was one of the original settlers in Wilcox County, Ga. and as I stated had a very large farm, which we thoroughly enjoyed.

One night, one of my cousins woke us up with a finger to his lips to be quite. He led us out of the house and down the road to a neighboring farm where he proceeded to teach us how to steal watermelons. Those were the best tasting melons. Just crack them open and dig in with both hands. We never did get caught. This also is where I got lost in a cornfield. I don't know to this day how I ever got out of there but I remember roaming around under all that tall corn, crying, looking for some way out.

Another night we all piled into a car and went to the community hall to see a movie. The movie was "Birth of a Nation", the original, so you know how far back in the woods we were.

Toby McDuffie, my grandmother, was a tiny little thing but full of vinegar and really loved to fish. She would never go anywhere without taking her fishing pole and quite often would fix breakfast, set it on the table and take off for the creek, fishing pole in hand. Don't know if she ever caught anything but I bet she did.

I have kept in touch with these folks over the years and go to the McDuffie reunion in Fitzgerald, Ga. as often as I can.

GIRLS

It must have been sometime about this time that I became interested in GIRLS as I remember vividly having a crush on a cute little thing named Virginia. However, being bashful I never pursued that relationship even though we went all the way through high school together. I did date once I got to be in the ninth grade, but I never did date my first love.

I met her years later after we had all retired and we went to dinner a few times before she passed away.

Me, Joan, Clarice 1940

My 3 sisters 1941

1941 Class Edison Elem

Mom & 6 kids

Me Circa 1943

Rev. & Mrs. George W. Sellers

W. C. McDuffie Sr. circa 1930

Mom circa 1970

High School Prom

Hillsborough High School

ROTC 1st Lt. 1952

9th grade 1948

EGGNOG

When I was about 9 or 10 years of age one Christmas holiday Mom invited a teacher friend over for dinner with us. It must have been right after Christmas Day or maybe even New Years Eve. After our meal I remember the lady setting a large punch bowl on the living room table and telling us she was going to make eggnog for us. Now this was something I had heard of but don't think I had ever tried. We all watched spellbound as she mixed the milk, eggs, and whatever else goes into the concoction and stirred it up till it was frothy. Then with a smile and Moms eyes big as saucers, she pulled from her purse a small bottle of rum and proceeded to pour it into the mix. "Real eggnog" she exclaimed. It was good! I remember her name was Ms Tichner.

Secret Spaces

For those of you who were not there these little vignettes of a youngster are not chronicled in order as they happened. I was just too young to remember the dates, just the episodes and I guess ultimately, that's all that counts. I had mentioned earlier about hiding under the living room table when the air raid siren sounded but I failed to comment about the unusual view one had once under the table. You see, the table was very well constructed. It had about a four-inch edge on which the tabletop sat. That edge had a lip, which was only visible from under the table. Now as we all sat under the table waiting we could see all the food we did not want to eat that had been very ungracefully deposited on that lip under the table. Eventually Mom made us clean that stuff up although I do not think she ever broke us of that habit. I guess it's fortunate that most tables today do not have that little hiding space.

GAS AND FIRE

I would be remiss if I did not take time here to explain about the hot water heater that I mentioned much earlier in this expose. We were fortunate, or unfortunate depending on ones level of bravery, to have both a hot water heater and a space heater that were operated with gas. The major problem was with the hot water heater as it did not have a relief valve. Therefore the one who lit the heater was the one responsible for making sure that when they were finished bathing, washing clothes, dishes or whatever they turned OFF the pilot light. Now if one forgot to turn that darned thing off then as it got hotter and hotter all the pipes would start to make loud cracking noises and the tank of water itself would start emitting loud sounds. When this happened everyone was horrified that the whole place would go up with a loud BOOM as well it could. Someone had to turn it off. One night we were all sitting around the supper table eating our spaghetti when that old hot water tank started to make those horrible sounds. Fortunately it was in the good old summer time and the front door was open. I say fortunately because when that tank started banging my brother John jumped up from the table, dashed straight out the screen door and was on his way to the far side of the street yelling "It's going to blow!".

One of us bravely shut the thing down as every one else rolled on the floor laughing at the speed at which John had gotten out of the house. Sure this could have been very dangerous and I guess we were lucky that it never did blow up.

We do not believe that it was caused by the hot water heater but we did have a fire on the back porch where the heater was housed. I came home from grade school and the little room in the back of the house, which had the hot water heater and a breakfast table in it was dripping wet from being hosed down by the fire department. The house was smoky for some time and it was the devil cleaning up that mess. It didn't burn house down but I lost my favorite 'Teddy Bear' in that fire and to this day when I see stuffed animals in the store I look for a replacement for that much loved bear. I've never found one that even closely resembled it and guess I never will.

FIRST JOB

As most of us kids did back then, when I was big enough, probably about ten years old, I went to work to help ends meet. My first paid job was painting a roadside sign for a local Kiwanis club. A friend and I did that on the dirt floor of our old garage. That thing was solid brass and was heavy but we did a good job. At least we got paid. After that I looked into delivering the Tampa Daily Times and was awarded a route which was right in my neighborhood. In those days the paperboy would get an apple crate (they were solid wood then), cut holes in one end to slip a cut off broomstick through, and then position that under the handlebars of your bike. The papers would be rolled or folded up nice and tight, placed in the apple crate and delivered by throwing them from the bike as you rode up and down the street.

My major problem was that I did not have a bike! Luckily a friend of the family stated that he would co-sign on a note with me and he even drove me downtown to the local Schwinn dealer to make the purchase. Now I had never owned anything this expensive and of course never borrowed money to make a purchase. If it cost more than a dollar it was too much for me and I did without. Now, some 60 years plus later, I remember that bike cost fifty-seven dollars! It was really a beauty. Red with silver fenders, coaster brakes, steer horn handlebars and a real leather seat.

I will always remember the day as I rode that bike all the way home from downtown, some three miles, in a driving downpour. That was some way to start off with a brand spanking new bike but it couldn't be helped. Anyway there were many days in central Florida when I delivered my papers in a driving rain. After all, I had a job to do and a little rain never hurt. I prided myself in making sure that my customers always had a dry paper, even if I had to walk up to the house and lay it on the porch. I only had one dead beat and that man still owes me nine dollars. My route grew over the next two years to over three hundred people so I was able to pay off that bike debt fairly quickly and move on to better paying things.

MAY DAY

In the forties we still had a May Day celebration in this country and school children would learn to wind colorful ribbons around a tall pole making a beautiful woven pattern. Each school would send a team of weavers to the grand May Day festival usually held on the playing field of the fair grounds and everyone would come out for the festivities. It would be a grand day all over the U.S. That was stopped when the Russians began having their May Day, which is no more than a show of force to the rest of the world. Anyway along with the May Day dancers, each school would have a May Day King and Queen, which was the biggest thing you could be in elementary school.

All the teachers and the PTA did the voting in each school and you could only be nominated if you were in the sixth grade. Well I was a final contestant along with a kid named Raymond. Now I really didn't know Ray at that time, at least not very well, but he beat me out for this great honor: yet we became friends and still are to this day. What a great honor to be in the running for May Day King. I sure wish I could remember who the Queen was that year.

SAFETY PATROL

Sixth grade, wow I get a lot of memories flooding through when that year comes up. I had been elected by all the teachers in the fifth grade to be a School Patrol and stand at the corner to help the little kids cross. I was again awarded that honor as a sixth grader which resulted in only the second time in my life that I had to go to the principals' office to be reprimand (spanked) and I didn't even do anything wrong.

Yeah you say I've heard that before. It started as I walked down to the next patrol crossing as I usually did to walk to school with my friend Bobby. As I approached his position, our principal drove up and told me to come on back to school. I said ok, waited for Bobby to finish helping his last group of kids across and we both went straight back to school. Well that wasn't quick enough for 'Old Lady Cone'. She called ME out of class to report to her immediately and accused me of not minding her. Me of all people who never got into trouble. The more I denied that I had done anything wrong the more it became evident that she must have been mad at my Mom and was going to take it out on me. Mom always stood up for her kids, which wasn't always appreciated by "authorities"

So I got the 'THE PADDLE'.

How humiliating to go back to class with everyone knowing you had been spanked!

The other lasting impression I have of being a school patrol boy was at the end of the sixth grade year. The sheriffs' department would take all the patrols in the county out for a full day of picnicking and swimming at a local swimming hole called Ralston Beach on Lake Egypt. With my light complexion, blue eyes and blond hair I should have known to stay out of the sun or at least put some sun lotion on but I didn't and at the end of the day I was as red as a lobster.

The next day was graduation day from sixth grade and in the forties we were still dressing up and having a ceremony with all the families' in attendance. My white starched shirt was a real torture on top of that burn and when friends and family slapped me on the back or gave me a hug it was unbearable.

YBOR SCHOOL

As my mother was in charge of "before & after" school (a day care center), we spent one half of the fifth grade in a school that was primarily made up of Latin kids from Ybor City.

Ybor City is a community in Tampa, founded by V.M. Ybor in the early 1900's, to house Cubans who came to Tampa to work in the cigar factories.

I fondly remember a young girl there who had a beautiful singing voice and could sing all the popular songs of the day. She kept everyone spellbound with the quality of her voice. The one song I really loved to hear her sing was Sentimental Journey. I sure would like to know if she went on to sing somewhere as we all thought she would.

BULLY BOY

As with most boys in elementary school there were bullies to contend with and I had mine. I did not just have one. No sir! I had two that I remember very vividly. In the fourth grade I had a friend named Dickey. Dickey lived about four blocks from Emma Street and his parents had a small grocery store right on 15th Street. We played together quite often in the empty lots behind our house. Dickey was a fat little kid who liked to have his way. One day for some reason we were playing at his house and Dickey started in on me. It wasn't long before it had erupted into a small battle and Dickey was chasing me down 15th Street to my house where I ran inside crying to my Mother that he was going to "beat me up". My Mother took no sympathy with me and said "Well then maybe you need to stand up for yourself and maybe he will not do this again." Wow, was I floored. Mom wasn't going to protect me. That took a couple of minutes to sink in but when it did I turned, went back outside where Dickey was waiting to smear me on the sidewalk and I begin to back him down. In no time he was hightailing it home with me in pursuit threatening to tear him apart. Dickey never bullied me again. Sometime later Dickey died of a disease we had never heard of before: Leukemia. Back then there was no cure known for this childhood disease and for a long time I thought that I had done something to make him die. Mom got me through that one with love and counseling only a mother can give.

My second encounter with a bully was with a real bone fide, honest to goodness mean guy in the fifth grade. Now Jack was THE bully of the whole school.

He had failed several grades so was much bigger than anybody, including God. He walked with a swagger like all bullies do and it was rumored that he even smoked cigarettes. Boy now that was really bad. He was the real life bully that NO kids my age and temperament liked to have to face—ever. I do not know now why he jumped on me this particular day but he did and as we were at play during school we could not fight on the school grounds so he threw the typical challenge to me. "Ok I'll meet you on the corner right after school and whip your butt." and he used words like "butt" that nobody else would use. Now to me, this meant surely that I was scheduled to die right after school. But remembering what my Mom had taught me (of course she didn't have to face him) I responded, "Ok I'll be there". Scarred to death, knowing he was going to leave me in a puddle on the street, I gathered my two brothers up to have someone to carry my dead body home. We slowly trudged down to the corner of Cayuga and 15th Street, the appointed place of my demise. We waited and waited and waited but he never showed up—much to my relief. I honestly do not know what I would have done had he appeared but he didn't and I never asked him why or mentioned it again. As a matter of fact he became friendly to me and remained that way for as long as I knew him.

About forty years later I met him in a tuxedo rental store. He had been very successful in life and was outfitting his family for his youngest daughters wedding. People do change.

MATH BLOCK

Something that I believed shaped my future academics was an incident that happened in the fourth grade. We were studying China and a good friend and I had painted an extremely large mural depicting Chinese 'coolies' working in a rice patty which was to be used as a prop for a play that we were also learning. It was a coincidence, I'm sure, that a rather large collection of jade from the Orient was on display at the University of Tampa and the class was going to take a bus to see this artistic marvel. Well my teacher decided to tie a little performance in arithmetic to determine if you went to see the jade. I missed the cut off point by a point or two. My teacher would not let me redo the quiz nor would she consent to allow me, a budding artist, to go see some of the finest jade jewelry in the world. To this day I have trouble with math and I do believe it is from this embarrassing episode in my young life.

MOM

These incidents taught me something that remain with me to this day and I am always thankful to my mother for doing this. Mom always told us never to run from your problems because if you do they will never be solved or go away they will just be waiting for you around the corner and you will have to contend with them again and again until you take care of them. Also, as you take care of your problems, you grow within yourself and become a much better person than you were. It worked then and it works now.

Mom! Wow, what a lady! I have, of course, mentioned her throughout this remembrance but I need to tell you now about her to the best of my ability. First of all, she was "MOM" and you never, ever doubted it nor did you feel any need to question her because she was MOM. Looking back and looking at pictures I now know that Mom was a very beautiful lady and had been delivered a hard blow by losing the only man she would ever love, my Dad. To top that she had six young kids to raise at a time when women were either teachers, nurses or secretaries. Mom was different at a very early age, as she had gone off to North Carolina or somewhere to school after high school when girls just did not do that. She became a teacher and taught in the elementary school where we went but not at the time we were there. After Dad died Mom had a day care school at home and during the war she was asked to establish what became known as the "before and after school" project. This kept elementary school children at school before and after the regular school time in order that mothers could work in the ship yards and other places to help the war effort. Mom also started the first ever, that I know of, day care center in the Tampa projects located on Lake Ave. At that time the projects were only for poor white people and I do not think there were any colored people living there. Mom always taught us kids that we should do the right thing and to accept what we did if there were repercussions and to learn from our mistakes. She apparently taught us to love and respect books as all of us kids love to read and explore through books. There was never any question in our minds that Mom did not love each and every one of us equally, as she would be there with a hug if needed or with a switch. I remember her as always being very level headed and I do not believe that any of us realized that we were poor until after we were older and on our own. Help was accepted but paid back. Bills were always paid and food was always provided. Mom taught me the value of buying quality goods as they wear better and last longer. So, to this day, I always try to shop around to find the best items I can for the best price.

Mom never purchased a car after Dad died and would always ride the bus to her job as secretary of First Methodist Church in downtown Tampa where she spent twenty-seven years before retiring. Over the years I have met many people who knew Mom from that bus trip. None of those people ever knew that we were struggling to keep our heads up and food on the table because Mom was always so positive and personable, ready to help anyone who may have needed it. I have no idea how we made it through those years without going on welfare but that was not a word that ever crossed my ears. We all learned to work together as a family and to help out financially in any way we could. If there was something that needed to be done, it got done or bought and we just tightened our belts a little more. We never went without.

I now know why Mom always had a tired look about her. That look was not one of sadness just one of someone who is constantly fighting to keep up—not necessarily to get ahead. That look could be and often was, lost with a big beautiful smile that came so easy and still does even though she is now eighty seven (at this writing) and not in the best of health but doing ok. It is difficult to put down on paper any one time that Mom set me down and had a heart-to-heart talk about anything. She probably did not have the time to do that with six kids. But I do know that my heart-to-heart talks were a continuing thing and as the circumstance demanded the talk was given on the spot and a learning experience took place. So my bringing up was done on a constant basis. I do not know how she handled it and us. A full time, demanding job and six kids. Only now, many years later, do I fully understand the frustrations, fears, heartbreaks, self-denials and joys that my Mom went through to raise us kids. She always put us first and her needs second; always had faith in our dreams and us and was always there to help us with our heartbreaks; never telling us what to do but helping us talk through things to our own conclusions. Then giving us the support to follow through. I know that through the years I have never really told Mom that I love her but I am trying to do that now at a time when she needs us kids. She has provided us with strength, fortitude, compassion, kindness, love, consideration for others, thirst for knowledge and above all a feel for fair play which I hope I have passed on to my children as part of her legacy to me.

Hazing Jr. Hi.

We were warned about our first day at junior high school and even though it wasn't as bad as we anticipated, the long summer of looking forward to the razing had its affects. As we approached the school grounds we were set upon by the 8th and 9th graders who all had multiple tubes of their sisters' lipstick or just a ten cent variety from the dime store for the main purpose of seeing just how much they could cover our faces with. It wasn't too much longer that we were as red faced as one could be. I had to ask Sis how to get it off once I got home.

I remember well sitting in the really large auditorium and listening to the principal tell us how we were going to behave and then assigning us to our "home rooms". I drew Ms. Lund as my home room teacher and that turned out great for me as she was an art teacher and I did like art. Our room was located in a small building detached from the main structure of Memorial Jr. High which turned out not much fun if it was raining or cold. Then the walk to the main building was out in the open.

PRE SCHOOL ANTICS

Not too many memories of junior high remain but some that shall always be in the back of my head. One such incident was on a gorgeous school morning. All the kids were standing around talking waiting for the bell to ring when a friend, "Pokey", called all the guys around him to tell a "off color" joke, which we were prone to do. After about 20 of us guys encircled him and he was standing in the middle of this circle when he suddenly shouted at the top of his voice "RAPE". You never saw so many guys scatter that fast in your life. "Pokey" stood there laughing.

PHYSED

Phys.Ed was always a joy for me as I loved to play touch football and was pretty elusive if ever given the chance to carry the ball. I also developed my love for basketball as I was not only fast but also quick. I remember many times when I would avoid the bigger players by my quickness or simply pass the ball between their legs, scoot around them and pick it up on the other side. I was not a great shot and did more team playing than what is called today "hot-dogging". I never did like baseball as I could not keep my eye on the ball to hit or catch it. I avoided that sport mostly. I believe that if we had played soccer back then, I would have been very good at that as I had quickness and good coordination.

LIBRARY

The public library was right across from our junior high school. We had to pass it on the way to school as well as coming home. I often stopped in and checked out several books for my reading pleasure. I never have developed a like for textbook reading but enjoyed the classics such as "Last of the Mohicans" and "Call of the Wild". I well remember walking to school when it was blistering cold with a wind whipping down on us. We had about a mile to walk to school but it wasn't a problem for us kids. When we got to the public library though, it was wide open space and that wind would freeze us to death.

The only kids that rode a bus were from Sulphur Springs, which was then in the country. To us they were "different" because they did ride those big yellow busses in.

TEACHERS

We had one teacher, nick named "Rumble Seat Sally". She was an older woman with an apparent spine deformity. She drove a small car, a Morris Minor I believe, and to the excitement of all the kids in School, one day that car wound up in the main hall of the school. To this day I have no idea who did that but it really was a scream at the time. My English teacher, Ms. Burney, was one of my special teachers. Even though she was very thin, I thought she was just beautiful so I paid attention in her class. Unfortunately I paid more attention to her than to the lessons as I still cannot conjugate nor do I do very well with all the English teachings. I could care less then if a verb (whatever that meant) was plural or used as an adjective and so on. I do get by now but am careful and read things several times to make sure it makes sense. I think that all the reading I did has helped me in this light as I feel I am fairly articulate. I do very well remember having to give book reports. I HATED doing that. I am an introvert and could no more get up in front of a class and give a report on a book than the man in the moon. So, I made a deal with the teacher: I would design and draw a book cover for any book instead of giving a report out loud. This got me through that portion of English very well as I loved to draw.

DIRTY TRICK

About this time, girls came into being. One in particular that ALL the guys were chasing was Gail. Now Gail was one of those blondes with a big beautiful smile and personality that just sparkled. She attended the same church as I did and we were friends but I wanted more than that like all the other guys. One problem Gail had was that she knew she was a knock out and she was very flighty. I could never get her to give me any attention except when she wanted something. So, one day I said I would get back at her. This is something that I've never been fond of doing as I am not a mean person but I was so frustrated with her lack of interest in me that did something that I found to be very humorous at the time.

Gail loved to chew gum and always had a mouth full of the stuff. I was employed as a delivery boy and soda jerk at a local drug store and went in every morning to open the store. On this morning, I purchased a box of "Chiclets" chewing gum, you know the little squares, and also a box of "Exlax" which looks just like the chewing gum and is a very good laxative. I switched the ingredients in the boxes and first thing that morning at school when Gail asked if I had any gum, guess what she got. I can only imagine what went on that day as she popped about 3 pieces in her mouth. I never told anyone.

My secret!

MORE GIRLS

I never had a girl friend at this age except Dorsey Lee. Dorsey Lee went to the same church as I did also but lived on the south end of town which was and still is the money end of town. I had such a crush on this girl it was unreal. When she would walk into a room I would get this big rush and get very nervous. Sometimes I thought I would blush if she looked at me with those beautiful eyes. I do not think that to this day she is aware of how I felt. She went on to marry a football star from her school, which I understand ended in divorce as he had a drinking problem, and I lost track. Dorsey Lee was thin but well figured and had the most beautiful eyes. Regular "Doe Eyes" and she was just a down to earth sweet girl. I did have a crush on another girl in the ninth grade. I finally got up enough nerve to ask her to go to a movie. I was surprised when she accepted and we rode the bus to the Tampa Theater. She only talked about the guy she liked and his motorcycle so that killed that crush for me. I think I liked her because she was blonde, had nice legs and wore stockings to school. That was sexy to me. Girls were the main topic of conversation among us guys and we did all the crazy things guys will do at that age to attract them. Sometimes successfully but most often not.

NEW STUFF

As I went into junior high WWII was recently over and the atomic bomb was a big topic. Items like ballpoint pens were being more widely used rather than the pen you could insert in a bottle of ink and draw out ink into the pen for writing. We all had the little blue blob of ink on our shirts from wearing the ball point pens in our pockets. I guess this is where the little plastic pocket insert came into play so as to not destroy a perfectly good shirt. Radios were being produced that you could put a battery in and take on picnics or anywhere else you wanted to. I remember having a small, by standards then, pink portable radio that had an antennae in the handle. The handle could swivel around so you could pick up the radio frequencies better. Girlie magazines were the ones we hid from Mom. Guess all us guys had those at some time as well as the National Geographic, which really showed more of a female, than we should have been looking at. At least according to morals then. But we did enjoy looking at those half-naked women even though they were African.

STARS

Movie stars, now that's where we could really lose ourselves, in a good movie. I loved the musicals especially. All those fantastic costumes and leggy women were better than the girlie magazines. Betty Grable, Dorothy Lamour, Mitsy Gainor, June Allison, Doris Day, Elizabeth Taylor, Betty Hutton, and of course Jane Russell in "The Outlaw". John Wayne was coming into his on then. Gene Autry, Roy Rogers were our cowboys and of course there was Robert Mitchum, the bad boy, Clark Gable, Henry Fonda, Jack Lemon, Red Skeleton, Bob Hope: and there were those wonderful singers; Bing Crosby, Pat Boone, "Ole Blue Eyes" Frank Sinatra, Hank Williams, Patti Page, Patsy Cline, Rosemary Clooney with "Comona My House", those swing bands that are history. Tommy and Jimmy Dorsey, Guy Lombardo, Glen Miller although he had disappeared during the war his band lived on. Xaviar Cugot, Gene Krupa with drums you could listen to.

We had stars then that did not demand to be international icons but just wanted to get on the big screen and we enjoyed them. We didn't have to be exposed to them every day as though they were what the world just waited to hear about. We had crooners then not people that get up and scream at you with words pronounced so badly you can't understand them or noise they call music. We had dancers like Gene Kelly and Fred Astair & Ginger Rogers that made you want to get up and dance and not roll around on your head or break your pelvis with jerking motions.

SNEAKING LUNCH

The high school was right across the street from our junior high and we all longed for the day we could be over there. One thing we were not allowed to do was go off campus for lunch but you know how that goes. There was a small diner just back of the exercise fields which served the best hamburger you could find (the diner is still there as I type this but has changed hands many times over the years. It is probably the only one of it's kind left in Tampa.) We would all band together and go for hamburgers when we had the money. It was easy in large groups. That way the principal or assignee could only catch so many of us and they tried. There was also an ice cream shop, "Langs"—that had the best home made ice cream in town.

Cars were very scarce then as most did not own one or there was only one in the family and Dad drove that to work. We guys pretty much used our bikes to get around or took the bus for dates if there were any dates.

CHANGE

I remember well the final stages of junior high and particularly the 9th grade assembly where each class had to get on stage and depict in some way what you wanted to do in life. I went on with shorts, T-shirt and basketball as I wanted to coach. That never came about!! As I sit here, the whole 3 years of junior high are just a blank. Maybe as I continue on something will strike a chord and a flash of memory will come back which I can record. I do remember that as we were getting ready to go to Jr. Hi. We were informed that we would be changing class rooms for each subject. This was a big deal as in elementary school you stayed in one classroom for all your subjects. We were sure we would get lost running around looking for the next class. But as it turned out we didn't.

AFTER SCHOOL

My life outside school was not all that interesting, at least it didn't seem to be to me anyway. I would go to school and to church and MYF (Methodist Youth Fellowship)but I was not active in hardly anything else. There were about 4 of us who would all ride our bikes to Raymond's house and then all walk on to school. Those guys have remained friends all theses years. Don't hear much from them but we do chat occasionally.

Buffalo Ave. Drug Store

Summers, for me, were spent working as we had very little in the money category. I began working at the Buffalo Ave. Drug store as I went into high school and worked there for all three years of high school. I started out by delivering prescriptions and sundry goods on my bicycle. I would go in first thing in the morning, sweep the store out, change out the water in the coke machine and add ice. Now there was a great piece of equipment. The "Cokes" would be put in and then covered with ice. When you wanted a "Coke" at Doc. Causeys' it was so cold it stung your mouth. Wow, that was really great when you were a boy. We didn't have air conditioning then. We had a little lady who worked behind the soda fountain that was as thin as a rail but had big eyes a wonderful smile and really was great for a young guy to talk to. Eddie was a smoker and would take breaks every once in a while to step outside and smoke. When she would do this I would step behind the soda fountain and help customer as best as I could. I did have a crush on Eddie, the older lady soda fountain person. There was just something about her that really made me like her probably more than I should. She taught me how to make different concoctions and eventually helped me give up the delivery end and become a full time soda jerk. This was fantastic for me as I love ice cream and could help myself as I liked. This was also a gathering place for the "drug store cowboys" in the area and I became friendly with a number of them that soon went off to Korea. It was also a super place to met the girls as they all came from the community for sodas or other sundry goods and would spend a few minutes talking. Being very shy with the girls I don't think I ever dated anyone from there. This job paid me $15.00 a week, good money for a kid back then. I was able to buy my own clothes and pay for school expenses with little drain on my Mother's budget

SPORTS

I longed to play sports in high school but always felt that I had to earn a living so never went out for anything. I loved basketball and track. Still do and even volunteered, in my junior year, to compete against St Pete High School to run the mile. Our track coach had come into my ROTC class looking for milers as he didn't have anyone from the junior class to compete in that event. I had never participated in a controlled race in my life but volunteered. I was given a pair of running spikes, normally worn by a sprinter, and started running to get in some kind of shape. The big night arrived. The milers were called out and off we went. Needless to say I was holding up the tail end of the group along with another classmate. We did get the crowed on their feet by racing to see who would NOT be last. I lost. My one and only high school sports competition. But it was exciting and I did go on to run many road races later. Then there was the annual Thanksgiving Day football game between arch rivals, Hillsborough and Plant. It was always held at a neutral location (Plant Field in downtown location adjacent to the University of Tampa).

The guys would buy their girls a Mum corsage and it was really one of the major social events in Tampa, at least for high school kids. Hillsborough almost always won those games. Another rival, well there were only three big high schools in Tampa for Caucasians as we were segregated, was Jefferson High. We usually beat them also but in my junior year (if memory serves me correctly) we were beaten by them due to a single player named Rick Caseres who went on to play many years for the professional Chicago Bears. As I have mentioned, track was always my favorite sport and when possible I would go to the meets which were held at Hillsborough's quarter mile track.

MORE GIRLS

Girls normally were the main thoughts of many of us young guys and I was no different. I had met Evelyn by this time and we went together through most of high school. The first time I ever saw her was at a Halloween party that my good friend Bobby had. We were sitting outside around a camp fire in his yard when this beautiful little dark haired girl comes walking over from the yard behind his. She smiled and I was lost. What a beautiful person to walk into my life. I fell head over heels right then. I would meet her at her locker in the morning, walk her to her classes and then walk her home after school. She only lived about six blocks away. Then I would ride my bike to work. Any dates we had, which were usually to a movie, I would ride my bike to her house, about a mile and a half from home, we would catch the bus and go downtown. Of course we all went to the football games. Usually the guys would all get together to go to the game and then go circle around the drive-in looking for girls to talk to or just pull in and have a burger and Coke. One memorable date with Evelyn was the night we went to her 9th grade dance. I shall always remember dancing to the strains of "Tennessee Waltz" that night. On the walk home we stopped under a street light and I had my first kiss from her. Still vivid in my memory!

HIGH JINKS

One night we were driving through a residential neighborhood and one of the guys had some firecrackers. We decided to have a little fun. The firecracker was lit and as it was tossed out the car window I screamed", No! No, don't shoot me!" The firecracker popped at just the right second and we squealed out of there, burning rubber, just as though a gangster had shot someone. We rode around for about 3 or 4 minutes then slowly drove back through that neighborhood. We really had a good laugh as every porch light was on and everyone was standing in their doorway. Another night we had come out of the Tampa Theater in downtown Tampa and on the way home, as we came to a stop light, we would all jump out of the car and stand there looking up at the sky. Soon all the pedestrians would start doing the same thing. We would then get back in the car and leave. Silly fun. Just like squirting people on the bus with a water gun. Busses were not air conditioned so the windows would be open. As we would drive by the bus, we would point our water pistols at the windows and squirt, squirt. Then turn a corner and get out of there. Just pranks that kids do and no harm was done to anyone. Just a few wet shirts or blouses. One Friday night after one of our football games, a group of us boys went to the downtown drugstore for Cokes. We sat in a booth in the back, played songs on the juke box and really were having a good time laughing and cutting up as we were prone to do. Apparently we weren't to appreciated by the rest of the clientele there. The manager came back and after several times asking us to be quite, he just politely ushered us out the door.

Another night after my friend Ken had driven his girl friend home from church. After we dropped her off we were on the way home and passed a nearby golf course. Now Ken was the proud owner of a little

Nash Rambler(I think that was what it was called). It was so small it stood out on the street. We decided it would be great fun to ride the golf course which we proceeded to do for about 10 minutes. Up one fairway and down another, till we figured we'd better skedaddle from there.

Extra Curricular

I was very active in my church, First Methodist of Tampa, and would take the bus to church every Sunday morning and night. The youth group was fairly active and I participated more as a follower than a leader. We would take summer trips to Leesburg (Florida) Youth Camp and became a very close knit group. I also became active in De Molay, a boys organization sponsored by the Masons. I really liked this and worked my way up to Senior Councilor before leaving high school and going in the service.

As a member of the DeMolay degree team I won a place on the all state degree team at competition in Jacksonville. I still have the medal I won. It was a very important thing for me as I was such an introvert.

One of the activities I was active in during high school was the morning worship service some of us held. After we were told that the school would not allow our private group to meet in school, we moved the service across the street to a Lutheran Church where I was active in Boy Scouts and were very successful in having that group grow.

Scouts would meet once a week and I worked my way up to Life rank, never tried for Eagle. Why? I have no idea. Guess I was destined to never seek the top spot as a youth. I well remember one scout meeting when we were to be tested on our observation. Each scout was led into a room that had ten articles in it. We were given about 30 seconds to memorize what was in there then immediately tested when we left the room. One by one the scores were given out getting lower and lower and I thought there's no way I would have failed that. Finally my score was given: the only ten in the group. That has always stuck with me as I am very observant of what is around me. Scouting was such a pleasure for me and I enjoyed the hiking trips and the working for merit badges. I became an assistant Scout Master when a senior in high school.

HIGH SCHOOL TEACHERS

My home room teacher, Mr. Steinberg, was also my Latin teacher. I have no idea why I took Latin except that I needed a language for college prep.

There was a well known factual saying around the school that you didn't want to sit in the front row of his class as he spit when he talked. It was true. I, like probably every other guy in school, was in love with our art teacher.

Young and vivacious, she had a great smile and twinkling eyes. I took art for one semester and that was all I could squeeze in.

Math was always a trouble spot for me as I had a hard time comprehending the word questions. It was the only subject I took that I did have to go to summer school between my junior and senior year to bring my grade up. I think math was the only subject I ever failed.

I use to walk to summer school with a classmate, Marge, and we became good friends but I lost track of her after graduation and many years later during one of our reunions it was said she had a crippling disease and had passed away.

One class I took as an elective was speech. I knew I wasn't good at talking in front of people and hoped this would help me. I did enjoy it and did fairly well but still had that fear of speaking up. We were required to give verbal assignments such as reciting something from Shakespeare and I could do that and even give it a little drama rather than just saying the words. Had I thought about it or even been aware of the possibility, I may have gone into acting. One event I will always remember is the day in woodworking that a friend almost lost a leg, or worse yet, his manhood. We had been very carefully instructed by Mr. Cates, our teacher, exactly how to use all of the power equipment in the shop. We were constantly advised about safety and how to correctly use all the power tools as they could be very deadly. But there is always one who gets in a hurry and doesn't pay attention. This day it happened to a good friend of mine, Dave We took woodworking class together as an elective.

He was using a radial arm saw, which required you to pull the spinning saw blade toward you. As he was doing this he wasn't paying attention or looked away from what he was doing and pulled that saw blade right into his groin.

Yep, he was out of school for a couple of weeks and just barley missed his chance to not become a father.

FRIENDS

It seems that, like most everyone else, I had a small group of close friends that hung around together and at lunch we would all sit at the same table rather than mixing except for those guys that had a "Sweetie". They would go sit with her for lunch.

The halls were always alive during breaks between class and I usually would quickly go to my girlfriends' locker just to say hi as she changed books for the next class and walk her to class. Many years later when I called her on the phone to renew our friendship, to my horror, she didn't even remember me. Looking back, that was really a nice time for me and one I think about more than anything else in those three years: the exchange of friendships during the day.

R.O.T.C.

I really enjoyed my ROTC classes and was moving up the ranks pretty quickly. In my senior year I was being considered as a captain along with another classmate. I lost out to him and finished up as a Lieutenant instead. Many years later I was told that the only reason he beat me out was that his mother was active in PTA and of course my mother had to work and was never active in any of those things. I have tried to reconcile that but am still working on it. He did go on to become a career military guy so guess that worked for the best. This training did help years later when I was serving in the army. I knew how to take a rifle apart, all the marching moves and more about military regimen than the other recruits so I moved up fairly quickly to NCO rank in the three years I served on active duty. I was given the opportunity to go to OCS (Officer Candidate School) but turned it down. One thing I never understood in the service was why they put the smallest guy at the end of the squad and I had to practically run on a fast march. Another memorable evening was the annual ROTC ball which was held at the Univ. of Tampa Auditorium. That was really a sight to see all the guys in uniform with their girls in evening gowns. I am not a good dancer and was NO dancer then but did manage to make it through the night. It was mostly slow dancing then and with all the girls in evening gowns, very little fast dancing which was fine for me.

As the Korean war was in full swing, our ROTC classes were very important to me and every Friday we would have to wear our khaki uniforms to school for drill. I was always proud to wear that uniform and tried to conduct myself in an appropriate manner. We wore starched shirt and pants with a crease you could probably cut bread with. Belt buckle shinning like the sun and shined shoes you could see your face in. I really enjoyed that and the image I thought it gave.

We had a drill Sgt., Sgt. Ansley, who was regular army assigned to us. I really like that man. I remember that as we were marching and someone happened to look down at their feet he would immediately say "They are no money down there or I would have got it". That is a direct quote that I remember to this day. This always brought a smile to my face and still does as I remember him. I understand that he was one of our casualties in Korea. A good man and a good solider and I say that with conviction.

SENIOR PROM

The big night that all seniors in high school look forward to is the senior prom and this writer was no exception.

I had dated Evelyn all through high school and was excited about taking her to the prom as she was such a beautiful girl.

The thing then was to buy your date a corsage which she would wear on her gown. In my preparing to buy her corsage I needed to find out what she was going to wear and of course what color the gown would be so as to not have clashing flowers. It turned out that she would be wearing an off the shoulder lavender colored gown so I would need to get her a long corsage as it would have to be attached to the strap on the shoulder. I told her I was getting her an orchid but she asked if would get an Iris instead as that was her favorite flower.

I of course accommodated her and the flower matched perfectly. I believe the Iris was white with a lavender edge and was just right. As she had large "Doe" eyes and dark hair she really was a gorgeous young lady and I was very proud to have her as my date. I know that we double dated with my good friend, Don, and his date as he had a car and you just don't take your date to the senior prom on the bus.

The prom was held at the Crystal Ball, a dance room located on Bayshore Blvd. in South Tampa. We went somewhere afterwards for food and drinks.

I was going to leave right after graduation to go to Tennessee to work with my uncle in Knoxville. I did the right thing and broke off with Evelyn just after graduation as it would not be fair for her to be tied to someone so far away or at least I think that is why. We were on good terms and I remember talking to her on her porch while we were swinging about my leaving.

I eventually attended the University of Tennessee for one year then went into the service and I never saw her again until after I retired and found out she was a widow. I made contact and we had a few dinner dates. She is still the pretty gal I remembered in high school. I must have just been gun shy from my recent divorce and was afraid I might get serious. I did not continue the relationship.

GRADUATION

I will always remember our graduation service as we were the first in many years to hold it on our athletic field.

The parents and family sat in the bleachers and the graduating seniors came from the gymnasium and filed into their seats on the playing field. All day we had expected rain. As the ceremony progressed, so did the dark forbidding clouds as they well do in Florida in the summer time. As the benediction was being said there was a crack of thunder and we knew it wouldn't hold off too much longer.

Now in June in Florida it is a big question mark to hold anything outside of this nature as the rains do come in on a fairly regular basis. True to the area, the storm gathered and it got darker and darker. As we were marching off the field, lightening begin to flash across the sky as if we were being pre warned that life is not easy and you need to prepare yourself.

We did not get wet but it was a very memorable evening.

HILLSBOROUGH HIGH SCHOOL

This school is very important to the city. It was the first high school in the county and was first located just north of the downtown area. As the city grew it became necessary to build a new high school and the current facility was opened in 1926. Many important figures in Tampa's history have walked the halls of old HHS and it was considered, one of the most beautiful high schools in the country.

The current campus, built in the middle 1920's, is situated in an area called Seminole Heights.

Its' design and construction reminds one of buildings you may see in Europe, with red brick exterior, a clock tower and spacious lawns.

The halls are all terrazzo floors and as there was no air condition then, each class room had windows that go from about waist high to the ceiling and open outward for ventilation.

Lockers for books and personal items were built into the sides of the halls. Each floor provided enough space for gatherings on each side of the hall for chatting between classes as well as room for foot traffic down the middle.

The school is equipped with it's own athletic field as well as a quarter mile track with bleachers and tennis courts.

As most students did not have a car at their disposal when it was built, there was very little parking area on the school grounds

Even today in the year 2012, it is still considered one of the most beautiful high schools in the country.

Northtown Theatre

Located on the corner of Buffalo Ave. (now M.L.K. Blvd) and Nebraska Ave was the local movie theatre. This was only some eight blocks from home and in easy walking distance. Every Saturday, as all across America, a youngster could go sit in the movie house for most of the afternoon and be entertained.

The cost was only about fifteen cents to get in and then candy or pop corn would cost another nickel so it was not all that expensive.

We (my sister and brothers)would all walk together except for the baby and Mom would keep her home.

Every Saturday would bring a new chapter in what ever serial movie was current like Nyoka of the Jungle, Queen Sheba, Tarzan, Our Gang the latest Pathe News Reels on the war and the world in general. Of course there would be at least one western with the Lone Ranger, Gene Autry, Roy Rogers, Tom Mix, Hopalong Cassidy and sometimes a real musical that would last at least an hour and thirty minutes. Every showing had several cartoons which we all thoroughly enjoyed. Popular was Popeye, and Loony Toons. Some of the best war movies were Back to Bataan, Guadalcanal, Shores of Iowa Jima and of course the spy movies about the Germans.

CUSCADEN SWIMMING POOL

The summers here in central Florida do get very hot. It is always nice to be able to go jump into a nice cool swimming pool.

It was not generally accepted back then for everyone to have their own swimming pool. As a matter of fact, there were very few home owned swimming pools then. These were limited to the really rich and there was none of those in my neighborhood for sure.

Cuscaden, was a city owned pool, located on the outskirts of Ybor City and about a good mile from our house. We could either take the bus on 15th Street or just walk to it which we usually did with our swimming suits all wrapped in our beach towels. Once there you would pay your fifteen cents, you would get a numbered tag on a band, with a key to a locker, you put on your wrist or around your ankle. After changing to your swim suit you would then walk through a shower and a foot bath of water and up the stairs to the pool.

This pool is really big with a deep end on the east end and wading pool opposite. The shallow end was about three feet deep. Then in a separate area was a really shallow pool for little kids about maybe three inches deep.

It was here I probably learned a lot of the Cuban or Spanish curse words that I should not repeat. A lot of the children using the pool were the children of the local cigar workers children who would utilize the pool. Ybor City and Tampa were known world wide for the cigars made here. Most of those factories were here in Ybor City.

I remember this pool well for the crystal clear water and the fact that I could swim about the length of it under water. I never did become an excellent swimmer but am not afraid of the water and can keep myself afloat well.

There was a tall chair at several locations where the lifeguard sat and they had life preservers they could toss to anyone needing them. They also had a long pole with a crook on the end to grab someone and pull them out of the water.

I loved to go here to swim and of course look at all the girls in their swim suits. Swim suits for girls were mainly one piece and the two piece ones were worn by some girls but they certainly were not the skimpy things you see today at the beach.

The Oak Tree Market

As a junior high school student I obtained a job at the above market and worked there for maybe 2 years. My job was varied, including cleaning cold drink bottles, and placing them in their respective containers. Each bottling company had their own wooden crates with a place for 24 bottles. Each crate was filled then stacked ready for the route man to pick up and replace with a like number of filled bottles. I checked merchandise on the shelves and made sure they were all dusted and added to if items had been sold. I swept the store daily and also delivered groceries to our customers. I used my bicycle and the same apple crate I used to deliver newspapers to place the grocery bags in. I don't remember having to ride very far to deliver but probably within a half mile of the store. The store was located on Nebraska Ave and only about six blocks from my house.